NKAZIMULO N. NGIDI

Me VS The World

An Autobiographical Novelette

Copyright © 2024 by Nkazimulo N. Ngidi

All rights reserved. No part of this publication may be reproduced, stored or transmitted in any form or by any means, electronic, mechanical, photocopying, recording, scanning, or otherwise without written permission from the publisher. It is illegal to copy this book, post it to a website, or distribute it by any other means without permission.

First edition

ISBN: 978-0-7961-8083-4

Editing by David Hughes
Advisor: Nompumelelo Moyo

This book was professionally typeset on Reedsy.
Find out more at reedsy.com

Contents

1	Foreword	1
2	Preface	3
3	Acknowledgement	7
4	Chapter 1: Where It All Started	9
5	Chapter 2: Coming To Accept What I Didn't Want To	16
6	Chapter 3: It Was All A Dream	20
7	Chapter 4: I Thought I Knew Better	26
8	Chapter 5: The Coming of an End	31
9	Chapter 6: Life On Thin Ice	35
10	Chapter 7: Letters To My Loves	44
11	Conclusion	50
12	Afterword	57
13	About the Author	60

1

Foreword

Dear Heart,

To my sweet heart:
That turns to the same page and plays the same melody again as the sun rises,
Heralding the start of a new day,

The light could be very bright;
But my heart is lost in darkness and no light can find it,
Even when the birds are singing joyfully;
No melody can move, dance, or win my heart,

You can see that I am inconsolable,
Paralysed, and drowning in my anguish,
With my cries constantly ignored,
Getting swept away by the rushing waves of my anguish;
Lastly buried in a mess I produced,

Thus, when the call to curtain rises,
And the sun gets ready to set,

> *I stay there, still motionless, drowning and immobilized,*
> *I wait for the song to repeat after pausing it,*
> *Because my life is told in that manner.*
>
> *- Nompumelelo Moyo*

* * *

I have selected this poem to be published as an extract from the poetry book written by one of my close friends, an exceptionally talented writer. I completely agree with the body of literature asserting that a foreword penned by the book's other author has more weight.

As mentioned above, the poem was supposed to be a part of an anthology my friend wrote sometime in 2021, with plans for me to be the co-writer. The title of it was agreed to be *Letters To Us*. Unfortunately, that never proceeded further for several reasons. The book would also be very different from a typical anthology in that it would include short stories in addition to poems, not only poems for flavor.

Like this work, it is divided into two literary genres: fiction and non-fiction. To be clear, I am not changing the rules of literature in any way; rather, I am making space for other writers to write in a way that is natural to them, without feeling constrained.

In addition, I revised the aforementioned original poem (with the author's permission) for this book.

Let's go right into the book without further ado.

I wish you a pleasant time reading the book.

2

Preface

I had begun writing this book long before I finished the last word. If my memory serves me right, I started writing this book in 2021. I lacked the courage to carry on. I think all I was missing was **The Platform** as I eventually came to terms with the reality that I had a lot of stuff I needed to get off my chest.

This inevitably reminds me of the 2019 movie [1]The Platform (chuckles.) A fantastic but underappreciated movie with a captivating cast and production. In a nutshell, it revolves around approximately +/- 500 strangers who awaken in a "Vertical Self-Management Center" consisting of 333 levels, each of which is partnered with two people and is shuffled monthly.

The levels are chronologically ordered, ascending from the highest to the lowest numbers. The kicker is that each level (room) lacks the basic amenities in a room setting. Each level has a common toilet, two single beds on opposite sides, and simply one washbasin for the two occupants.

You are not given any money, entertainment options like a TV, or anything besides food once a day, and you are certainly not allowed to leave The Platform

---

[1] https://www.imdb.com/title/tt8228288/

until your time is fulfilled, which could be anything from 3 months to a year.

Every month is unique; everyone is given a drug for one night and rendered unconscious to be moved to different levels within the platform than the one they were previously on. This is all coordinated by "The Administrator," which is another name for the facility owners. Once again, you are paired with a different person every single time you are drugged and shuffled.

Believe me when I say normal prison life is a luxury compared to the vertical platform's prison life. Let me tell you why: during your time there, "The Administrator" hires the best chefs from around the globe to prepare food for people inside the facility. The Platform is filled with all kinds of food (from starters to main dishes & desserts') and all the refreshments (including alcohol) you can ever think of that travel via The Platform, level to level (capped at 2 minutes on each level.)

Anyone can have as much as they want—a buffet of their own, you might say—as the platform goes from the highest to the lowest numbers. However that inevitably leads to conflict, as the residents at the top levels get to eat as much as they can, with each level only getting the leftovers from the previous ones. With the core rule that you are not allowed to 'SAVE' any food for later; if you did, the level you are on would either get too cold or too hot (unbearable); in essence, there was no 'I'll eat later'.

Some individuals would eat as fast as they can, as much as they can, then spit, s#it, or do some despicable things to the food. Justifying it with the fact that in other months, if you are unlucky, you would one day wake up on level 40, with the platform reaching your level, with the food finished, or even worse.

Push would come to shove if that's the case, and one would end up killing and eating their roommate because they were "hungry." In our traditional language (IsiZulu), we say, "Indlala ibanga ulaka" translated to "hunger breeds anger" in English.

My point is this: I was hungry for emotional belonging and a sense of being for such a long time that I started consuming many unhealthy foods. I'm referring to accepting love & treatment that I felt & knew I didn't deserve, which ultimately led to me using drugs at some point in my life and having multiple suicide attempts because my soul was not satisfied. Just like in The Platform.

No matter how much food you consume in one day, that doesn't count towards your hungry days in The Platform. The same thing happened to me. I used to stuff myself with as much junk as I could get, but that never counted towards my soul remaining hungry the following days.

* * *

This book might resonate with some individuals, and it might not with others, which is completely fine. *Edward Parnell* said something so interesting in his book, "*Ghosted*", He said,

> [2]"*I don't believe in the vacuous concept of 'closure'. You can't get closure. Sure, there is some catharsis, but it is also upsetting. I'd be writing this stuff thinking, 'I'm not sure I should have written that'. On reflection, I think it was right to do.*"

Luckily, or unfortunately, I share the same sentiments. Stories tend to go longer and longer—usually because we are interested in the subject matter—which can lead to parenthesis, goose chases, and interconnected storylines. We wind up limiting the range of our own life experiences as a result of our minds trying to protect us from the trauma that may arise from our own experiences. We either tell someone about those events or just put them in writing in an attempt to relive them.

---

[2] https://www.amazon.com/Ghostland-Haunted-Country-Edward-Parnell/dp/000827195X

Not because I am weak, on the contrary, I feel stronger than ever, which is why I am choosing to be vulnerable. I have no idea how or where I will be on an emotional level when I complete this book, but if you are reading it, I do not doubt that you will read it as though I were sitting down with you and sharing a story.

I want you to feel all the sensations I felt when writing this book, because, in my sharing of my life experiences with you, it is not my job to tell the story that they (society) want me to tell; I'm telling a story, that is, a story that has made me who and what I am today.

3

Acknowledgement

Even though my parents aren't bookworms like me, I still hope this book makes an impression on them. I want to thank them from the bottom of my heart. I treasure you!

And also to my brothers. I appreciate your unwavering support, even during my trying moments.

I would like to sincerely thank my cousin Pride, my friends Amanda Mkhize and Nompumelelo Moyo, and myself for always believing in me.

Siwelenkosi, I am grateful for your goodness in my life. Above all, even after 2.5 years, I truly thank you for your forgiveness. But even if you say you've forgiven me, I know there may still be emotional scars. Despite my errors, I hope you can still love someone else the way you loved me.

I am indebted to Herbert Scheubmayr for his unwavering friendship and invaluable assistance in the publication of this book!

[3]David Hughes, it was an honor to have you swiftly edit the book because you are a very skilled and experienced writer. Most importantly, I would like to thank you for exposing me to the [4]Ikes & Collectables Bookshop community.

In Chapter 5 of this book, I will also talk about the relationships that I am trying to mend. Temahlubi Dlamini, I appreciate you letting me be your buddy once more very much. As the saying goes, people come and go in life, but only true friends—of which you are happily one—stick in your heart. I'm hoping it will thrive rather than wither away.

---

[3] https://ikesbooks.com/products/st-pauls-anglican-church-durban-an-official-history-by-david-hughes?_pos=4&_psq=david&_ss=e&_v=1.0

[4] https://ikesbooks.com/

Chapter 1: Where It All Started

This has had to be the hardest thing I've ever had to do—of all the tasks and challenges I've faced in my life—but since I've already begun writing this book and feel like I've overcome half the obstacles, I've chosen to take it on.

I honestly feel proud of being a Cancerian because it is one of the traits that have helped shape who I am today. I was born under the Cancer sign. For those who are unfamiliar with astrology or "star signs," let me explain that the word "cancer" comes from the Latin word "crab," which is our zodiac sign. In addition, summer in the Northern Hemisphere and winter in the Southern Hemisphere, which spins about June 21 to July 22, begins with the Cancer season.

The energy and hearts of those born under the sign of Cancer are said to be shielded. To keep ourselves secure, we frequently conceal our true selves beneath the allegory of hard shells, much like a crab shell.

Nurturing and loyal, Cancers are also protective of their loved ones. While reserved, we stand on a foundation of strength and aren't afraid to act when necessary.

The crab symbol offers a key to understanding cancer's preternatural ability to know things without understanding how we know them. Crabs wander about at night, crawling sideways. Due to our sideways march, we can observe and see life from an alternative perspective than others. In the sign, this translates to creative, artistic, and intuitive minds with the power of (sometimes psychic) perception.

With Leo as the King, Cancer is regarded as the Queen of the zodiac signs as they are currently known. Let's simplify it to my life. I've spent my entire life—now 26 years—living in my shell, believing that if I stayed hidden from the outside world and its problems, I would be safe. To be honest, I've been stalling my development.

* * *

Although I was raised in Emafakatini, Pietermaritzburg—the capital and second-largest city in KwaZulu-Natal, South Africa—I was born in Durban on **July 14, 1998**. The town I was raised in was named in 1838 and is currently governed by the [5]Msunduzi Local Municipality.

More significantly, the town of Pietermaritzburg is called after uMgungundlovu, the royal homestead of King Dingane (eMakhosini). Up until I was a few years old, I lived in Pietermaritzburg with my paternal grandmother, my father's mother. Even though my grandmother was elderly, I recall that she would carry me on her back as we walked great distances to and from home when I had chicken pox. She had no other choice because our family was not affluent and our home was located in a remote area.

My parents were struggling at the time, working incredibly hard to provide for our family, and I was too little to realize what was going on. To cut a long

---

[5] *Msunduzi Local Municipality.* (2024, May 24.) Wikipedia. https://en.wikipedia.org/wiki/Msunduzi_Local_Municipality

tale short, everything worked out just perfectly. I had to move back to Durban and live with both of my parents in a flat in the Durban CBD area until I could remember, which was an improvement over what I had previously witnessed.

Regretfully, I had to move to Cabhane, Mtwalume, Port Shepstone to live with my maternal grandmother. Umtalumi, another name for Mtwalume, is a community in [6]Ugu District Municipality in the KwaZulu-Natal province of South Africa—a small seaside village, predominantly a holiday and fishing village.

During my time in Port Shepstone, my family decided I was too smart to wait until I was eligible to start school, and as a result, I was enrolled in Grade 1 and passed my academic year with outstanding results. I was not even 5 years old, but I am not there.

My parents believed it would be wise to move back to Durban, South Africa, to live with my maternal grandmother. Kwa-Mashu is a township located 12 kilometers north of Durban. I had to start preschool again in 2003 at David Landau Pre-Primary School, and then I had to enter Grade R at Roseland Primary School in 2004. I had no idea that would end up working in my favor down the road. As a child, I had to swallow my pride and embrace the changes because I had moved three times in five years.

You know, you grow up with the same mentality of thinking and deciding what's good for you and your close companions without taking into consideration their feelings and thoughts when something happens to you as a child and your parents do what they think is right by not sitting you down to explain some things.

Let's not focus on that though. It makes sense; I've learned to turn my parents'

---

[6] *Ugu District Municipality.* (2024, May 31.) Wikipedia. https://en.wikipedia.org/wiki/Ugu_District_Municipality

mistakes into principles. Lord knows I would have responded to the same or very comparable scenarios.

Before we could proceed further, I was informed of the death of my paternal grandma in October 2007. My understanding of death was limited due to my young age, but I remember feeling deeply saddened and sorrowful. Grannie, who looked after me when I was unable to, loved me beyond words. She used to call me "Stimela Samampondo, 1218." For those who don't know, "Stimela Samampondo" is one of the first few prophets of [7]Ibandla lamaNazaretha, South Africa's second-largest African-initiated church. Using the nickname "Stimela Samampondo" to make fun of me, my grandmother compared my big head to the archetypal head of the prophet from ancient Nazareth.

* * *

In 2009, while I was in Grade 5, I became ill, and my mother took me to McCord Provincial Eye Hospital (which was known as McCord Hospital until 2014). My diagnosis from the doctors was HIV/AIDS, most likely from birth. I never accepted it, no matter how much my mother, the doctors, the nurses, and the counsellors attempted to explain to me what was going on and how my life would change from that day on until a cure was found (if at all.)

I attended a weekly support group for all infected kids until 2010, when I had to move to Isipingo, a town situated 19 kilometers south of Durban in KwaZulu-Natal, South Africa, which currently forms part of [8]eThekwini Metropolitan Municipality. I had to live with my mom's identical twin.

Let's rewind just a bit. The eldest offspring of my grandparents were my mother, **Nomakhosi Maria Msimang,** *and her twin. My uncle, Robert, who will be our term*

---

[7] *Nazareth Baptist Church.* (2024, June 8.) Wikipedia. https://en.wikipedia.org/wiki/Nazareth_Baptist_Church

[8] https://en.wikipedia.org/wiki/EThekwini_Metropolitan_Municipality

for him in this book, is the next oldest of my uncles. In a news flash, mom shares her birthday with South Africa's former President, [9]Nelson Rolihlahla Mandela. The way mom and her twin used to jokingly rub it in my face that I was born 4 days earlier, God! (chuckles.)

My mom is a foundation phase teacher who loves love and appreciates life.

She graduated from a Bible college in the 2000s and has been preaching the word of God ever since. Talk about a God-fearing Christian. I know her prayers have saved me from a lot of negative forces. I love my mother to bits and honestly, I could never ask for another mom.

Nonetheless, My mother's twin (name omitted) has 2 children: my half-sister (a year older than me) and a half-brother (2 years younger than me.) My mom has just me and my brother (11 years older than me), from different fathers, as her only 2 children.

Now that's out of the way, let's continue. So I lived with my mother's twin for exactly a year and returned to Kwa-Mashu because I was *gatvol* (tired.) I won't take away the fact that I had one of the best times in Isipingo.

It was 2010, and it had been declared that South Africa was hosting the 2010 FIFA World Cup. And what's the best way to celebrate that with your mother's twin and your siblings? All nations united in one spirit, and it felt good every day. Remember [10]Waka Waka by [11]Shakira? Man, it was a time to be alive!

The thing is, my mom's twin would accuse me of things I supposedly did wrong, like misusing food supplies, and would constantly remind me that I

---

[9] *Nelson Mandela.* (2024, June 7.) Wikipedia. https://en.wikipedia.org/wiki/Nelson_Mandela

[10] *Waka Waka (This Time for Africa.)* (2024, May 31.) Wikipedia. https://en.wikipedia.org/wiki/Waka_Waka_(This_Time_for_Africa)

[11] *Shakira.* (2024, June 5.) Wikipedia. https://en.wikipedia.org/wiki/Shakira

was nothing and that she took me in as a result of my mom not being able to take care of me because she's a failure.

Top of it all, she would hint to her children, with me present, that I'm inferior because of my status. And believe me, that wasn't what fumed me up; it was the fact that she was my mother's twin. Because I was still in Grade 6, I couldn't just abruptly leave in the middle of the year (regardless of how I had enough of it.) With that still happening, taking the ill-treatment as is, I would do all the chores I was assigned and eat at Robert's house, which was luckily opposite my mom's house.

Get this: I don't blame my siblings (mom's twin children) for keeping quiet about anything that was being done or said to me in their presence; I mean, they were also still young, like me.

Nonetheless, I held on to my daily routine for months before I had my mom fetch me in late 2010, when the academic year was over. There's no question that I made it & passed Grade 6, regardless of where I was emotionally.

> *If you are reading this, mom (the twin), know I forgive you. Luckily, my grandmother taught me that forgiveness is never given for the other person's sake but for your own. God always keeps track of everything.*

In addition, I completed my seventh-grade education at Kwa-Mashu's Khethamahle SP School in 2011. Through the after-school program *Soul Buddyz*, where we were coached by Ms. Fraser (RIP), I rapidly befriended Sizwe Ayanda Ndlovu (RIP) & established my first infatuation with Amanda Mkhize, my present friend (laughs). Imagine having constant butterflies in your stomach. Frankly, I was eager for break time to meet my crush.

I was a member of *Soul Buddyz* not because the school mandated that students be on the team, but rather because my teachers thought highly of me for my intelligence and, lastly, because of my childhood and my regard for educators and students in my age group and below. They used to conjecture rather than encounter it that often.

5

Chapter 2: Coming To Accept What I Didn't Want To

WOO-HOO! High School! Where dreams die or are conquered (if you know, you know.)

Nonetheless, the reason I said that is because I still feel shocked and heartbroken when I see that some of the brightest minds we had in both primary and high school now street kids or into drugs. Worse, mentally insane.

I'll tell you now, free of charge, that most peers my age that I come across today have their lives turned around in the blink of an eye because of one or two (or all) of the below factors:

1. They were disrespectful towards their educators or peers in school.
2. They were disrespectful towards their family members when they were growing up.
3. Neighbors or family members had cursed their lives because they were rude and disrespectful beyond a bearable level.

Respect is really important. Not only do you respect those who are older than you, but you also appreciate those who are younger.

CHAPTER 2: COMING TO ACCEPT WHAT I DIDN'T WANT TO

* * *

Let's follow our book timeline in sequence. Where were we again in 2011? Yeah.

(We'll call him Sipho.) In 2012, I was pals with a high school acquaintance at Nqabakazulu Comprehensive High School in grade 8. Okay, so Sipho and I had a reputation for being the cleanest boys in the eighth grade, and we truly were. It's reasonable to say that I changed when I began smoking cigarettes (I can still clearly recall the brand, Craven A) and got into two relationships in a single year. That's when the problem began.

At home, my aunt gave birth to twins. The rest of the family, including my grandmother, and I, were thrilled for her. After the twins were born, my grandma and I had to take care of them because my aunt was preoccupied with other matters. Every day after school, I would either help Granny prepare dinner for the entire family or feed the twins, bathe them, or get them ready for bed before starting my homework. We took turns taking care of those chores with Granny, and finally, I ran out of time to support my smoking habit.

Unfortunately, in May of 2013, my grandmother and a few of my family members got involved in a severe car accident heading to one of our families in Ladysmith, which is a city in the [12]Uthukela District Municipality in KwaZulu-Natal, South Africa, for a family ceremony. Due to her uncontrollably high blood sugar levels, my grandma was unable to survive.

They say a woman can turn a house into a home with just her presence. I can very much attest to that because, ever since my grandmother passed away in 2013, our home in Kwa-Mashu has never been the same. The warmth is gone.

---

[12] *Uthukela District Municipality.* (2024b, January 1.) Wikipedia. https://en.wikipedia.org/wiki/Uthukela_District_Municipality

One thing about grief is that it might manifest suddenly if not properly cared for. Shortly after my grandmother's funeral, I went back to smoking cigarettes. One thing I will always remember about my high school life is that the teachers adored me, including the principal, which led to my joining the debate team as early as 2013.

As the youngest learner to be part of my school's debate team, I couldn't tell my peers, at least not until I was eligible as per the school requirements. Later on, in 2013, I passed grade 9, with Sipho on my side.

My class teacher, Ms. N. Mbanjwa, ensured I got into the physical sciences stream the following year, following my academic marks in Grades 8 & 9. I started my grade 10 but somehow hung with the wrong crowd and started smoking marijuana. I passed my grade 10, but not as I envisioned, and because I could feel it deep within my veins that these were not my marks. I told my parents. But in a fabricated manner. I decided not to go to grade 11, but rather repeat grade 10, and change my studies to suit me & my lifestyle.

I give thanks to God for giving me the perseverance and faith to watch my friends—including Sipho—graduate to the following grade. After my grade 10 performance went well, I continued with my musical career and initially focused on hip-hop, but later I moved into music production and deejaying. I could easily balance my academic pursuits with my musical aspirations.

In addition, I completely regained my former academic spark in grade 11, ranking second in geography, top five in biological sciences, and the best history learner overall.

I was selected as the senior debater for our debate squad by my school in 2017 because I could swap sides in contests without preparing. Soon after, I launched an after-school tutoring series of measures to assist my fellow 12th-grade classmates in the subjects of geography, history, English, and biology. That was a huge success because more students—mostly from private schools—joined my sessions from other schools. I was more flabbergasted than just middlingly happy.

However, I had to design a more accommodating method, which finally led me to acquire past national exam papers for revision. I was regrettably mugged three times in a single calendar year as a result, but my mojo persisted. In any case, I easily completed my matriculation, and it was now time to go from high school to the real world.

Chapter 3: It Was All A Dream

Rather than going on, allow me to share one of my 2019 imaginary short stories & I'll add another after every two chapters to liven this up. I'm hoping you like them!

* * *

It Was All A Dream

> *"You'll meet your match one day, I'm not wishing bad luck upon your life but I'm just reminding you of what you already know but choose to be ignorant about. Karma catches up with everyone. Have a good life, thank you..."*

I said this to Lizwi in a text message. I waited seconds, minutes, hours, days, months, and months for his reply until a year and 3 months went by and I eventually healed.

It took me precisely one year and three months to fully recover, and he dared to return a month later, keep calling, and offer *at least* a friendship, but when

CHAPTER 3: IT WAS ALL A DREAM

I was completely engulfed in love, where was he? When I sobbed several nights because I missed him, where was he? *At least*, where was he when I was hankering after him? When I hoped he would stop coming to the mall with the females he assured me not to worry about when we were still together.

You may be asking yourself why I detest him so much. I'll take you back to the moment I believed I was in love with the man, but in reality, I was in love with the balaclava he was wearing. Born on **August 24, 1998,** my name is **Nomagugu Zulu.** Yes, I am a born free, but if you were to see what I've seen, you'd probably go blind.

My amazing friends always make me feel better by calling me Nomah, and I adore them for that. My family has seen me grow up, but let's just say they don't know anything about me.

I attended a criminology lecture at the Howard College campus of the [13]University of KwaZulu Natal, where I met Lizwi Ntanzi, as silent as a button on a mute box. I didn't have a choice; I initiated the conversation before you said anything. I needed a refresher on the material presented so far in the lecture because I was running a little late.

> "Uhhhm Hi, have you been here since the lecture started?" I asked

> "Well hi, there Miss and no, I just got here too, like a few minutes ago, I'm Lizwi by the way."

His voice quickly won me over, but I didn't want to reveal my identity to him, so me being me, I just said,

> "Okay, ngiyabonga" (Thank you)

---

[13] *University of KwaZulu-Natal.* (2024, May 26.) Wikipedia. https://en.wikipedia.org/wiki/University_of_KwaZulu-Natal

Smart, right? (hahaha)

* * *

We only had criminology on Tuesdays and Fridays, so I only got to (sometimes) see him occasionally because the campus was always busy and I wasn't the always walking around type, not because I was smart, no, quite the opposite. I was simply lazy, which is very typical, I know.

Okay. I was just more interested in walking with my thoughts than my feet; I wasn't entirely lazy. When I return home, I normally pour myself a cup of coffee and stash my books in my wardrobe before lying in bed for a while and reflecting on my day. Yes, I fold my day that quickly. History is what's left. That's how, exactly, I ran out of time to think about boys.

* * *

(Days Later)

"I noticed you didn't tell me your name the other day, hi"

Startled by this whispering voice in my ear, I turned to face him.

"Lizwi am I right?"

I asked as we both entered the lecture doorway. To my surprise, he just chuckled and went to find an adjacent seat to mine and sat apart from me. Smh.

Moreover, he was on the steps outside the lecture hall as soon as the lesson ended.

"I saw where you were seated and came out fast to wait for you outside

> before you disappeared, as always after class. Let me reintroduce myself, I am Lizwi Ntanzi" he said

"Well. I am Nomagugu and what do you mean by "you came fast to wait for me outside before I disappeared as always?"

He just laughed and said,

> "I'm running to a meeting, but I would like to explain that. If it's okay with you, I'd like to talk more about what I meant over coffee maybe this weekend or whenever you have some spare time."

> "Plus, I also don't see you around campus very often. You seem to spend most of your time thinking deeply about everything or reading books on science fiction, astrology, or the end of the world (laughs). In any case, you require a break, and I won't accept a no."

I simply laughed and forgot; I even had a psychology lecture immediately after, and I gave the dude my number (to a phone I even forgot I had.)

Long story short, we went for coffee and coffee, and ultimately I fell in love with him, but he just loved me (at that time, I thought he was also in love with me.)

Everything started smoothly; he showed me off, and I showed the world why I was happy and why he was simply the source of my happiness. What strangest and most depressing aspect of love, in your opinion? In a relationship, you never know how deep or shallow the water may be until you jump in. You are only looking for the pleasure you desire, drawn in by the smiles you observe on people's faces, but you have no idea what lies on the inside.

* * *

Okay. He posted a photograph of himself and a female in a photo session on WhatsApp, and that sparked our first major argument (yep, he was a model). You know how it bothers us, girls when our men get too cozy and too close to a particular girl? Yeah, I had that vibe too. I asked him about it and you know that one thing you dread your man doesn't say in an argument? Yes, he did say it, and I was taken aback by how casually he stated it.

> *"Babe she is my model friend, don't worry about her, she wouldn't even be a threat to you, even if she wanted"*

(Like, who the f*** does he think he is?) I eventually began to doubt my sanity, but I handled it coolly until I could not. I regret sending the lengthy message to confront him because I was afraid it would make him seem even more distant than he already was.

The truth is that, when a relationship ends, we as women tend to place the blame on ourselves before fully reflecting on the situation. Fears that we have include disappointment, rejection, heartbreak, unhappiness, and, in the end, fear of men and, ultimately, fear of love.

All we want is for men to prove to us that men are not the same; all we want is for men to remain how they were at the beginning of a relationship, all we want is for men not to change; and finally, all we want is for men to keep their promises. Is that too much to ask?

* * *

Okay. Speaking of Lizwi and me, I started to hear rumors that he was having an affair. I didn't believe them at first, but I noticed that he was becoming less and less involved. He lied when I challenged him about it. I foolishly decided to forgive him since, I believe, my love for him was strong. I discovered evidence of his infidelity, sobbed over it, confronted him once again, and he issued an apology. Naturally, I extended my forgiveness to him once more.

Then, one day, I went to his modeling agency to surprise him because I started a new job for our June school break. However, when I got there, I saw that he was having an affair with one of the ladies that he had assured me not to worry about. I cried aloud because I was unable to control my tears. He came after me to say he was sorry. I wasn't thinking clearly, so I didn't hear a word. I had urged the cabbie to wait for us to go to the restaurant he loved, but I got into the cab and went home. That's when I wrote him a text message and it read,

"You'll meet your match one day, I'm not wishing bad luck upon your life but I'm just reminding you of what you already know but choose to be ignorant about. Karma catches up with everyone. Have a good life, thank you for all the heartbreaks, they taught me how to take care of my wounds, and thank you for the smiles and happy moments; they taught me how to get over the bull#hit the world constantly threw and still throws at me."

Love is a dream, like this story.

Because of my past experiences and the stories I have heard, I know that love needs strong people. And because of Lizwi, whatever the case, I met him in my dream, but I'm afraid to love or even consider it now. A friend once said, *"Emotional scars never heal, but they submerge."* That didn't make sense, but it does now that I have tons of emotional scars caused by one weapon, *love*.

7

Chapter 4: I Thought I Knew Better

Everyone reaches a point where they think they know 'better'. For me, that was in 2018. You might as well presume that I was fresh out of high school the previous year, and I assumed everything was going well, according to my plans and schedule.

Down the road, +/-5 years later, I understood that we (humans) 'plan' but God 'decides'.

Okay. So I was enrolled in one of the most prestigious universities in South Africa, the University of KwaZulu Natal, and to be honest with you, it was such an enrapturing feeling.

My majors were psychology & criminology, with my electives being English & sociology. Boy, I was excited to begin my lectures. I met a former high schoolmate, who was also enrolled at the same campus, Howard College, and we befriended 2 new friends; ultimately, we became a clique.

Fast forward, a few months went by, and I found myself selling pot (weed) to my fellow students and lecturers. I started to use intense drugs (cocaine) and more.

CHAPTER 4: I THOUGHT I KNEW BETTER

Then my clientele grew exponentially, and I increased my merchandise and added 2 more drugs to my supply: Alprazolam (a drug sold under the brand name Xanax, used to treat anxiety disorders and panic disorders) and different kinds of Lean (also known as purple drink, which is a polysubstance drink used as a recreational substance made with Codeine, containing cough syrup, occasionally alcohol, and the antihistamine Promethazine.) It's safe to say that I was a drug dealer on the school campus.

I hadn't neglected my studies at all. I had runners that used to sell for me. That was until RMS Security (Risk Management Services Security) got involved and found my stash of pot hidden, and luckily I was in a lecture (thank God for that.)

* * *

Back home, the situation wasn't conducive for me. With my aunt ill-treating me (more family dilemmas) and having meetings called every once in a while, it was no longer a safe space for me, at least not anymore. Long story short, my parents found a communal rental for me near campus, and I went to live there. Let us rewind just a bit on my father; I haven't talked much about him.

> Ooh. Talk about a genius. **Bhekani Richard Ngidi.** Well. I'm proud of my father. I mean, besides him being previously part of the [14]Police and Prisons Civil Rights Union (POPCRU) which is a trade union in South Africa representing police officers, traffic officers, and correctional officers. The man formed part of the team that drafted the South African [15]Labour Relations Act 66 of 1995 and played a huge role in the [16]SAPS

---

[14] *Home POPCRU | POLICE, SAPS, DCS, NATIONAL TRAFFIC. (2023, August 30.) POPCRU.* https://popcru.org.za/

[15] *Labour Relations Act 66 of 1995 | South African Government.* (n.d..) https://www.gov.za/documents/labour-relations-act

[16] *South African Police Service.* (2024, June 5.) Wikipedia. https://en.wikipedia.org/wiki/South_African_Police_Service

(South African Police Service) as we know it today. Without abandoning his homeland, he visited several nations on what I believe was a ten-plus-time tour as an acclaimed ambassador from South Africa. (I aim to beat him, I don't know how but I know I will.)

Both my parents are hardcore Christians and I've come to feed off similar traits (sometimes.) My father has two other children who are older than me, therefore we are his only three children, all boys.

* * *

Subsequently, I experienced a series of depressive episodes, primarily brought on by thoughts of inadequacy stemming from my social standing. But now that I think about it, my constant questioning is what was causing those resentful feelings. Like the ARVs I was taking and why I was taking them.

The thing is, I was 20 years old but still missing a lot of questions relating to my status, and my mom, who was supposed to be the answer to most questions I had, was not there. Look, I understand that she was probably trying to find her feet in this life as well, but I was also dying inside, day by day.

Moreover, I felt that smoking pot to think myself away was not working, as I felt like it should have. So what's the next thing I turned to? You guessed it right: alcohol. After that period, I saw no value in continuing with varsity, so I dropped out and immediately went to look for my first-ever formal employment at a call center in Umhlanga, Durban.

God finds a way to make it clear to you that The route that you have selected is not the best one for you. And he did, which is why I was mugged a few days after I was formally hired as I was waiting for transportation to work, but did I comprehend? Nope.

CHAPTER 4: I THOUGHT I KNEW BETTER

In November of 2018, I moved in with my father. A few months later, I felt I had obtained much exposure and introduction to the call center industry (worse, I had worked for a USA client, so I felt like an expert in the field, hehe), and it was time to jump ship.

Putting aside getting employed at a reputable call center in Durban, CDB, I met a very respectful, loving, and gorgeous lady, with the same designation as mine (for this book, we'll call her Siwelenkosi.) We kicked it off immediately with Siwelenkosi (Siwe for short), and there was no doubt we couldn't get enough of each other. We spent my birthday together, with my father present, and he liked her immediately (I could understand why.)

* * *

In October of the same year, me and Siwe decided to move in together, and it was an easy process, conducive for the both of us to be closer to work and to have all the time to ourselves (as we wanted.)

God still blessed me. I had the opportunity to be chosen among 3 other employees to be the face of the company in 2 of our (then) company locations. Returning to Siwe and myself, our employer appreciated our work efforts. Consequently, we received recognition from both our company and the client in months (one could say in a healthy competition, pair goals.)

I then took the most foolish decision of my life and chose not to disclose my status to her. I defaulted on my medication for a year until I got ill. Like a mother would look after their offspring (that reminded me of my paternal grandmother; younger, with chicken pox taking care of me regardless.) I fell into a deep depression and used the very same medication I used to sell back in 2018 as antidepressants. Naturally, that didn't work out, so I made my first suicide attempt, which Siwe discovered.

Unresolved emotional baggage tends to come back to haunt you at some point.

I didn't know that to be true, regardless.

I recovered physically and was able to stand again. I served as a junior team leader at work. In addition to my well-known hard work in my department, I was a subject matter expert for the entire international campaign I was working on.

I decided to flirt with other women (sometimes in Siwe's company) rather than clinging to the dime I had, and since I'm a guy, that didn't seem to upset me. She would find out on countless occasions, but instead of stopping, my ego would get stroked, and I would continue (thank God, I didn't go on and formally cheat on her.)

She had it with me on August 8, 2021, and I wholeheartedly supported her choice. We broke up, and being the jerk I was, I never went after her, and I'm sure she thought it was because I felt out of love or something. No. Sometimes, you hurt someone so much that you look back at how much that person held you down and how you constantly disappointed them. I am a living testimony that *'people never get flowers while they still smell them'*.

It was back to the drawing board, and I returned home to Kwa-Mashu and was on and off on my ARVs from 2021, but only got back fully in 2023 (I know, very foolish of a smart cookie like me.)

8

Chapter 5: The Coming of an End

It's a normal thing for people to regret some of the stupid mistakes they made in life; as you might presume, I did too.

That didn't matter, though; I had found new ways of bandaging my emotional wounds. I had new friends, and that only mattered in my life. Oh, and I didn't have time to stay where I didn't feel appreciated, so I jumped jobs like nobody's business. I finally landed a job at a new call center in Umhlanga (job number 3) in 3 years (yeah, I was untouchable.)

Moreover, I was now exposed to not just any UK clientele but motor insurance, so that went over my head, but I left after a few months. I'm not trying to justify my jumping ships, but back then, I didn't know any better; I failed to appreciate my parents and my gifts (and talents.) I wish you could try to point me in the right direction!

* * *

By 2022, I had moved out of home and was now living with [17]Herbert Scheubmayr founder and owner of [18]Jamesons Bar which operated at the Chelsea Hotel, Catherine Avenue, Hillbrow/Berea, during the 1980s, in Johannesburg, South Africa. Jamesons Bar moved to Durban and operated as LA Renaissance Restaurant, then Jam & Sons, and finally, Jamesons Pub, located between Anton Lembede & Dorothy Nyembe Street in Durban. Jamesons Pub became known as the hub of live performances & bands and later took the storm in the whole of the Durban area.

I was not only living with Hebert as someone who needed a place to stay as home was no longer conducive, but as a close friend and employee. I would do a stock take on an everyday basis, handle all things technical, and later on, found out that I had a passion for digital marketing. As a result, I completed an online course to become a skilled digital marketing strategist. After completing my online course in digital marketing, I took another online course for a diploma in psychology and passed that with ease.

Everything was running smoothly until I had too much to drink one day and smashed Herbert's car so badly (it had to remain on Jamesons Pub grounds for months.) I landed another call center job, outsourcing a cruise line, originally from Basel, Switzerland, with marketing headquarters in Los Angeles, California.

We operated in North and South America, the Caribbean, Antarctica, the Great Lakes, Europe, Russia, Egypt, China, and Southeast Asia with our three cruise line divisions: Ocean, River, and Expedition.

I once again made another stupid decision. Instead of utilizing my newly found

---

[17] Matwadia, E. (2021, September 23). *Why place matters in celebrating Jo'burg's club history*. The Mail & Guardian. https://mg.co.za/friday/2021-09-23-why-place-matters-in-celebrating-joburgs-club-history/

[18] *Log in or sign up to view.* (n.d.). https://www.facebook.com/groups/6673554466/

employment to my favor and saving up to pay for the vehicle damages, I fell into the trap of using drugs (Xanax) and went crashing (no pun intended.) In a nutshell, Herbert kicked me out of his apartment, which was rightfully the wise thing to do. Eventually, I stopped helping out at Jamesons Pub.

* * *

I had given up on life as we know it and believed I saw no reason to live. As you recall, I discussed 'our minds play tricks on us' at the opening of this book, assuming that it does that to keep us safe. My lifestyle at the time forced me to make changes, and my heart finally turned into a beast that even my parents could not recognize.

You know when you are trying to hold on and manage your life, but it seems as if life itself keeps throwing jabs at you? Yeah, I was there, and it's not a place I would wish anyone else to be.

2023 came as we knew it, and I decided to take a breather from work and amend some of the relationships I had messed up previously. Most importantly, I wanted to return to my ARVs and be consistent in that routine.

We connected instantly when I caught up with my ex-friend, turned girlfriend. A week before my birthday in July, we decided to give ourselves a chance, and I thought, "I found the one" and chose to disclose my HIV status to her. How I ought to have handled Siwe.

I don't know what got over me, but I felt my life was no longer worth it, I was depressed, and I attempted my second suicide attempt (luckily she found me right in time.)

Later, when I began to question her commitment, she unexpectedly confided in me, saying that, among other things, my unemployment made her feel like I was too much to handle. Some of her words pierced through my heart, but what was at the core of my pain was that I felt less of a man because her words made me inferior in every way possible, a contributing factor being my status.

I don't know if it's because my parents are hardcore Christians or perhaps I was given some supernatural powers (chuckles.) I can sense someone's aura and a change in the environment (spiritually.) I discovered that she had an affair with another man. I asked her about it countless times, and she eventually was forthcoming with me.

I forgave her, as far as she knew, but my heart was no longer in the relationship. One thing I don't forgive is cheating because I am disgusted with the thought, so someone doing it to me is beyond what I can bear. I know what you might be thinking right now, but Siwe, I know.

* * *

Moreover, I found a job as a radio personality at a community radio station in mid-December 2023. I worked as a digital marketing strategist and a radio presenter. Lend a helping hand to the radio station with ad hoc duties such as voice-overs, music production, sound engineering, and graphic design.

In February 2024, I decided to work more on growing my digital marketing agency while sticking to my regular monthly visits to the doctor for my medication. I worked on obtaining a laptop to employ for my clients, and in March 2024, my romantic relationship became a thing of the past. To be above board, I didn't get bumped as I thought I resorted to.

After 12 years of everyday smoking, I took control of my health by quitting my smoking habits. Alcohol included.

9

Chapter 6: Life On Thin Ice

N*kazimulo Ngidi* (South Africa) was born in **1998** in Durban, South Africa. A young narrator and author who grew up in a family of hard workers, educators, and intellectuals. He grew up with the mindset of learning to train one's mind and working as twice as much to reach a certain destination in life. He believes that upcoming generations in a family should be more qualified than past generations in every family.

In this short story, the narrator tells the story of a wealthy family of four: Mr. Simon Locksmith, Mrs. Terry Locksmith, their two children, Jay and Selena Locksmith, and the family dog, Teddy. Simon is suffering from the rare sickness of a heart murmur.

***

(At the hospital.)

"Nurse 1,2,3,. again, 1,2,3, it looks like we are getting our patient back, one more
      time!"

"1,2,3. it looks like we have him back (Doctor Ridge showed relief.)"

"Nurse please change the patient's drips, I'm going to look for his family", Doctor Ridge instructed

* * *

(In the waiting room.)

(Mrs. Locksmith stands and rushes to the doctor before the Doctor says anything.)

> *"Doctor, Is everything okay? Is my husband alive? What happened?"*

> *"Mrs. Locksmith, unfortunately, your husband is in ICU and we all are still running more tests on him but he will be okay, your husband is a fighter. We and other medical specialists are doing the best of our capability to..."*

> *"In ICU?!, If you are doing everything enough..."*

(Mrs. Locksmith breaks down in tears before she can proceed.)

> *"...Then (Pause) Then Doctor why is my husband sleeping like a corpse in an ICU hospital bed? Why isn't he here with his family? Tell me"*

(Terry cries even more.)

> *"Mommy, please calm down, the doctors are trying, dad is going to be okay and*
>   *please stop crying you are scaring Selena, please calm down", Jay said*

Mrs. Locksmith replied in a low voice, with hiccups accompanying her voice.

CHAPTER 6: LIFE ON THIN ICE

"Okay, I'm sorry. Doctor, please continue"

Dr. Ridge Continues,

"As I was saying ma'am, we are working to support your husband despite his critical condition, which is that he has a diastolic cardiac murmur. A diastolic cardiac murmur is a sound produced by the heart's rapid, choppy (turbulent) blood flow. Examples of these are whooshing and swishing sounds. Thankfully, there is a solution to assist your spouse. We can carry out a procedure known as cardiac catheterization, which is defined as replacing the damaged heart valve. This procedure is vital because if it is not completed as soon as possible, we may lose your spouse permanently"

Terry followed up,

"So, doctor, what's stopping you from replacing his heart valve as soon as possible?"

"It's not easy, ma'am. We've determined that a transcatheter aortic valve replacement is the best course of action, but regrettably, we've also discovered that your spouse lacks appropriate health insurance. Notwithstanding that the process is well known to be highly expensive", Dr. Ridge replying to Terry

(A deep sigh from Terry.)

"Jay, go buy ice cream with your little sister", Mrs. Locksmith reached for a R100 banknote and gave it to her son, Jay.

* * *

(The next morning.)

(Mrs. Locksmith is on the phone.)

> "Bill, I will sort out everything as soon as I get the power to do so, please hang in there"

In a bold voice, Bill replied,

> "Terry If you don't fix this, I will fix it, fix you and your whole family"

(Bill hangs up before Mrs. Locksmith replies.)

* * *

(Back at the hospital.)

> "Good afternoon, is Doctor Ridge in today?, if he is may you please tell him that I'm here for him?"

> "Good day to you too ma'am, name and surname please?"

> "Mrs. Terry Locksmith"

(The secretary checks the system.)

> "I'm sorry ma'am, it looks like you don't have an active appointment, would you like me to set it up for you?"

(Terry breaks down in front of the secretary.)

> "I know but I need to see him, it's urgent"

CHAPTER 6: LIFE ON THIN ICE

"I'm sorry but I really can't let..."

"It's okay Lauren, she can come through", Dr. Ridge politely instructed the secretary from the hospital hallway

* * *

"Doctor good afternoon, I came to check on my husband's condition, how is he? Is he getting any better? We are all worried about him, including his friends and close relatives", Terry expressed her worry to Dr. Ridge

"Well, ma'am, I wish I could give you a definitive answer right now, but our interdisciplinary heart team of specialists and cardiac surgeons are in Kenya performing operations. Unfortunately, because of the complexity of your husband's condition, we will have to wait for them for the following day or two", replied Dr. Ridge.

"I hope your team gets here before anything drastic happens", Terry sighed deeply

(Doctor Ridge showing confusion.)

"Ma'am, I'm lost, before anything drastic happens?" Doctor Ridge inquired

"Eh..hem (clearing her throat) It's nothing Doctor, I was just saying", Mrs. Locksmith replied

"Your husband is going to recover soon ma'am, we have him on our 24\7 watch", Doctor Ridge reassured Terry

Mrs. Locksmith just stood up and left Dr. Ridge standing like a statue

* * *

(Back at the Locksmith household.)

Well, just a brief background of the Locksmith household. For starters, the house is located in a high residential area made up of 12 rooms in total in the main house and a separate room outside the main house for braai purposes.

There is a garden boy, a maid, and an electric fence throughout the yard. There are two bedrooms for the children, a bedroom for Mr. and Mrs. Locksmith with a separate bathroom, two guest bedrooms, a dining area, a kitchen, a study, an entertainment area, a room with an indoor pool, and a basement. The driveway and garden are lined with black and grey asphalt, while the facade is powder blue. The inside walls are painted white, with Elf Oak natural laminated floors.

Mrs. Terry Locksmith holds a PhD in mathematical statistics and is a 42-year-old psychologist. However, the head of the household, Mr. Simon Locksmith, is a 46-year-old shipping and logistics CEO with a building business. The 19-year-old son of Jay Locksmith, a grade 12 student, and his 9-year-old sister Selena Locksmith, a grade 4 student, rounding up the list. The family drives a 4x4 Ford Ranger, a Mercedes-Benz V300D, and a grey BMW X5.

* * *

(It's day 2 and Terry just came from the hospital; the phone rings and is written, Bill.)

CHAPTER 6: LIFE ON THIN ICE

Terry ignores the phone and after a few unanswered rings, the phone backlight comes on with a text message from Bill and read;

> "I'm going to make your life miserable tonight if you don't make any move; you'll wish you kept the end of your deal. I know you are reading this message and intentionally ignored my phone calls"

(With Terry shaking, she put on her nightgown and went for a drive.)

* * *

(The next morning, the phone rings and Terry picks up shaking.)

> "H..e..y", Mrs. Locksmith answered

> "Good morning Mrs. Locksmith, it's Dr. Ridge, I'm sorry to wake you up but it's about your husband, could you please come to the hospital immediately?"

> "Doctor, what happened, is my husband okay?", Terry asked

> "Ma'am I can't speak at the moment, please come to the hospital", Dr. Ridge exclaims

Mrs. Locksmith hangs up and instructs the maid;

> "Mary, I'll be back right now, please take care of the kids for me", Terry leaves without waiting for a reply

* * *

(Mrs. Locksmith heads to the hospital and rushes to Dr. Ridge.)

"Doctor, what happened, where is my husband?", Terry asked with hiccups accompanying her

"Well, Ma'am, the team meant to operate arrived last night and had scheduled the operation for this morning, but sadly Mr. Locksmith didn't wake up this morning. I'm so sorry," Dr. Ridge said softly

(Mrs. Locksmith just burst out in tears that even a person in an ICU could wake up.)

"But you, you... you said he would be alright, didn't you? Then what happened?", Terry cried.

"Ma'am we don't know what happened, we had the situation under control, I'm sorry again", Dr.Ridge in reply

(Mrs. Locksmith ran out of the hospital in tears.)

* * *

(Back at the household.)

"Mary, are the children still at school?" Terry asked Mary, the maid

"Yes madam", in reply

"Okay, please wake me up when they are back, I need to tell them something, for now, I'm going to lay down in my room"

(A phone call wakes Terry up and it's Bill.)

"Eh..m hello" she answered

CHAPTER 6: LIFE ON THIN ICE

"Hi Terry, meet me at 3 PM at our usual spot and come alone"

Bill hung up before Terry replied.

* * *

(A harsh police door knock followed.)

"Mrs. Terry Locksmith?", a policeman asked

"Uhm yes"

"Terry Locksmith, you are under arrest for the murder of Simon Locksmith and the trespassing in a health facility, what you say can and will be used against you in a court of law"

(She was handcuffed and escorted to the police van.)

"Mary, please call my mother and apologize; I didn't mean to turn the machines off. I needed my husband's money to get out of the debt I was in due to my gambling addiction. I love my kids, so please ask Mum to watch them too". Terry gave the order.

"Yes madam, I will do that", Mary replied.

(The policeman shoved Mrs. Locksmith into the police van.)

Terry Locksmith was given a life sentence for the murder of Simon Locksmith, her spouse.

Money is not the root of all evil, but love for it is.

10

Chapter 7: Letters To My Loves

A letter to MY MOTHER

Mom. Where can I begin?
I mean, no one can ever understand nor grasp the level of love I have for you, not because you're my mom but because you love me that much, I believe so much in reciprocating energies, especially feelings associated with love.

This book (letter) aims not to show the world how much of an emotional wreck I am or even the deepest secrets our family holds. Rather, it's an invitation to any reader, to see how much your prayers, ever since I was born, have made me the tough cookie I am today.

With that said, there are some things I wish you could have done differently, as a parent, more especially as a mother.
As I said at the beginning of this book, using some of your mistakes as my principles is one of my coping mechanisms in life, and always has been.

Please don't take anything I said personally in the book (still yet to say.)

CHAPTER 7: LETTERS TO MY LOVES

In our IsiZulu language, we say, (ngizowakha, angizile ukuzobhidliza) translated to (I'm here to amend, not tarnish things) in English.

My status mom. I've waited 26 years for you to talk to me about it, or at least from 2009. I mean, some of the choices I've made, have been influenced by how I've seen the world from my teen years till date. I expected you to be able to talk to me at least about how I came to have this disease in the first place. I know you've been beating yourself up about it, trust me, it's been worse for me.

Regardless, I don't want to put everything into my status and make this about it, the decisions I've made in life weren't ALL driven by that.
I have been more foolish in my decisions than I can count,
More sloppy with my relationships than how I was taught,
That's certainly not how you and Granny raised me,
And for that, I am deeply sorry.

Moreover, I have seen how sloppy you have been with our relationship, as mother and son.
I hear from other people that you are disappointed in me, for DEFAULTING my medication, what medication mom?
Even worse from my father that I have DEFAULTED for +/- 10 years.
Honestly, that was painful to hear, not even a hint of how you were mad at me for that.
I mean, as far as I know, you've never played the part of explaining the reason why I started ARVs, ever.
I would have understood.

I wouldn't wish anyone, related or not, to go through what I've gone through.
I'm this grown, emotionally and spiritually because of you and Granny and I am appreciative.
The sacrifices you've had to make previously have turned out to be

blessings, trust me on that.

In as much as I won't dwell that much into what we have been through, together.
I want you to know this, I love you, more than you could ever think and I know I will make you proud, eventually.

Once again, nothing I have said (still to say) takes away the fact that I love you, I couldn't have asked God for another mother.

PS: I miss our relationship and quality time together.

* * *

A letter to MY FATHER.

I think about you, and what you have gone through, and my heart gets heavy every time.
With what I've seen and gone through, thus far in life,
I understand how hard being a man can be.
Especially if you have (an) offspring(s) of your own
You swallow your pride and do what's required, not what you think is right.

Having a role model is not all glitz and glamour.
It's about seeing past their flaws and how you would add your strengths, to be way greater in life.
Certainly, having a role model as a father is not easy because you witness some of their failures.

Trust this though,

CHAPTER 7: LETTERS TO MY LOVES

Some of the mistakes and wrong choices I've made previously are nothing compared to the blessings I am to reap.

The jokes we've both made about the lack of mom's emotional intelligence are;
Serious than ever.
However, you don't have to worry about my EQ because of the time we have spent together, you taught me better.
The life lessons you've given me are more valuable than the Holy Bible.
I know they come from a warm place in your heart.
And for that, I'm forever grateful.

Forgive me for being a pain in the neck at times,
I NOW have learned.
And I'm sure my brothers are proud of the man you ought to become,
Cause I am too.

I know you and mom will hear (read) some of the things for the first time and wonder, be angry, or have mixed emotions about them.
They are (were) not meant as any form of disrespect to either one of you.
I have apologized too much for my actions previously that I know you (probably) are now tired of listening to the same song, over and over.
These however will serve as official apology letters.

Moreover, you surely have traits of a father that I would love for other fathers to have.
Thank you for being a proud role model to have.
I love you pops (No homo) (chuckles.)

PS: Your humor has made a difference in people's lives, don't ever stop.

* * *

A letter TO SIWELENKOSI.

They say you save the best for last, right?
Well. I hope that's clear.

Out of all the women I've been with in my life,
Our time together was filled with so much excitement, love and adventure,
That I don't think I'm ever going to experience in my life.

Nothing I say NOW will right the wrongs, I made, BACK THEN.
And I know you've probably heard this (probably) before, from your ex's,
But I assure you, none have been as sincere as I am going to be.

I know I made stupid decisions, trust me, I wish I didn't.
I know I made you a laughing stock at work, at home, more especially where the feelings you had for me lived, in your heart.
You are the definition of a great woman and I've hated myself, for not appreciating that, while I still had it, in my life.

I had to lose you first to realize I had a diamond in my hand.
I've had people who knew about you ask about us,
And I didn't know how to answer without lying.

I know you are one of the people who;
read some of the stuff I said in this book for the first time.
Just know,
I positively meant every word;
especially about being sorry for everything.

You made me question if I loved you enough, countless times,

CHAPTER 7: LETTERS TO MY LOVES

And yet you loved me like no one ever loved a person they hardly knew,
And most importantly, you made me a better person, inside out.

I hope one day you'll find it in your heart to forgive me entirely,
Not because your forgiveness would mean so much,
But because I hope you can love again.

PS: Thank you for your love.

11

Conclusion

The last thing I would like from people, or, should I say, my readers, is for them to not feel sorry for me in any way. That would defeat the purpose of writing this book. All I know is that it's not a memoir, as far as literacy is concerned. You can think more of it as an autobiographical novelette, if there's even such.

***

According to [19]Pathfinder, in 2017, 65% of people lived with HIV in sub-Saharan Africa, making that 38 million people in the world, and 1.8 million people in South Africa.

---

[19] Taylor, J. (2023, May 15.) *HIV & AIDS - Pathfinder International.* Pathfinder International. https://www.pathfinder.org/focus-areas/hiv-aids/?utm_source=google&utm_medium=cpc&utm_campaign=hivaidspathfindercountries&utm_medium=grant&utm_source=google&utm_campaign=XX&utm_content=&utm_term=hiv%20statistics&gad_source=1&gclid=CjwKCAjwvIWzBhAlEiwAHHWgvbf2SB5j7XasEdT84NxGFfdfHU7bVTk_ClNh_0uwOtrnDtAROpWjixoC0lgQAvD_BwE

CONCLUSION

Thank God we have organizations like the [20]Bill & Melinda Foundation, [21]Stephen Lewis Foundation, [22]Elton John AIDS Foundation, and the [23]AIDS Foundation, with headquarters in Durban, South Africa, working towards the 2030 HIV/AIDS goal: to end the HIV/AIDS epidemic as a public health threat, within the context of ensuring healthy lives and promoting well-being for all at all ages.

As much as South Africa is known as one of the leading countries globally, with the most infected adults & children of +/- 7,6 million people, as per [24]UNAIDS. Those numbers are forecast to drastically decrease by the year 2030.

The reason I am bringing those stats up (I know there might be a lot of mathematics involved) is not to discourage infected individuals all over the world, but in my research, the reason why we have so many people, especially the youth, getting infected almost every once in a while is because peers my age (regardless of how they got infected) find it very hard to accept their status, given the stereotypes around the disease, social discrimination, and self-stigma.

Since March 2024, I started a movement, or should I say a WhatsApp group I manage daily. It gives people hope that things will eventually fall into place, especially for inexperienced individuals. The group is called **Call**

---

[20] *HIV.* (n.d..) Bill & Melinda Gates Foundation. https://www.gatesfoundation.org/our-work/programs/global-health/hiv

[21] *Visit the Stephen Lewis Foundation.* (2024, June 3.) Stephen Lewis Foundation. https://stephenlewisfoundation.org/?gad_source=1&gclid=CjwKCAjwvIWzBhAlEiwAHHWgvbSHp2YOr_D3KCGoZbfbXZqQhwDOBUg6S9_Dcc2QDYU1WFA6eFUhPRoC8xEQAvD_BwE

[22] *Get Involved - Elton John AIDS Foundation.* (2024, April 9.) Elton John AIDS Foundation. https://www.eltonjohnaidsfoundation.org/get-involved/

[23] *AIDS Foundation South Africa.* (2023, January 9.) AIDS Foundation South Africa -. https://www.aids.org.za/

[24] *South Africa.* (n.d..) UNAIDS. https://www.unaids.org/en/regionscountries/countries/southafrica

Centre Inquiries & Assistance. As I have highlighted above, one of our visions is to help unemployed people get hired by preparing them for greatness with everything anyone who has never had any formal employment needs, including verification of any jobs posted on any online job boards.

We have people who have never worked at any corporate place before getting hired, and we are currently sitting on +100 members already. The reason I mentioned this is that I somehow was approached by one of the group members on the side, with whom we had a very heartwarming conversation. She ended up disclosing that she has been living with HIV/AIDS for over 30 years and has ongoing life-threatening health complications. She is currently being treated at a nearby hospital.

I couldn't bring myself to tell her about my side of the story, but somehow it motivated me to make sure I unarchive this book from my online shelf and finish writing it, in preparation for self-publishing if push comes to shove. The matter of truth is that her boldness, forthcomingness, and honesty, especially with someone she barely knew, will forever make a mark in my life. I truly am grateful.

* * *

One of the key factors or drivers of this book is to let the reader know that whatever disease you might be prone to or have been medically diagnosed with, that doesn't have to determine the direction your life should take. No matter the situation you might think is beyond you right now, talking about it is better than self-containment, trust me.

This brings me back to my interview, or, to be precise, my employment journey over the past 5 years: I've never failed an interview or received negative feedback of any sort. Now, this is not to boast, but it has been my motivation from 2021 until date. Let me tell you how.

During, let's say, the first 2 years of my employment journey, I used to feel bad. I used to believe in positive criticism a lot. After re-reading the [25]law of attraction this time around with more understanding, I searched within myself to see if there was anything wrong with that, and to my surprise, there was nothing wrong, just a bunch of blessings.

Don't get me wrong; I am not saying that out of all the 10+ interviews I've had, I've been successful in all. What I'm saying is that out of all the jobs my ancestors and God have chosen to be beneficial for me, I've been successful in 8/10 of them. One would ask how, right?

It's too simple. **Your Mind.** What do I mean by that? Your life is the result of your thoughts. The good, the bad. Impossible?

Let's be practical about it and take President [26]Barack Obama, for instance. Do you think that during his time living with his mother and half-sister, [27] Maya Soetoro, in [28]Hawaii for three years from 1972 to 1975, while his mother was a graduate student in anthropology, he never experienced any highs and lows in life?

Broadening the spectrum, he probably experienced self-doubt and self-loathing in some way, but he prevailed and one day became the 44th president of the United States from 2009 to 2017. Isn't that something you now think he is proud of?

Going back to you and me, we might experience highs and lows, especially

---

[25] https://www.thesecret.tv/products/the-secret-book/

978-1582701707

[26] *Barack Obama.* (2024, June 9.) Wikipedia. https://en.wikipedia.org/wiki/Barack_Obama

[27] *Maya Soetoro-Ng.* (2024, May 31.) Wikipedia. https://en.wikipedia.org/wiki/Maya_Soetoro-Ng

[28] *Hawaii.* (2024, June 7.) Wikipedia. https://en.wikipedia.org/wiki/Hawaii

in our mid-20s, which may influence how we envision our lives to be in the coming years. However, those negative and self-loathing thoughts should never be above the positive thoughts you have ever had of yourself to date.

"Why not? I mean, I can't control that, especially my thoughts." One would say that.

Well, I am here to tell you that one can control their thoughts. Dr. Barbara Fredrickson's extensive research reveals that we need three positive thoughts to balance the power of one negative thought. Exceeding this 3:1 ratio is key to happiness, productivity, and effectiveness, even in group and corporate interactions.

I might not have everything I have ever dreamed of right now, but I assure you, writing this book from 2021 has given me so many broader perspectives on life, including on the law of attraction and how to apply that in my life. I hope reading this book as well gives you similar sentiments to share.

* * *

I might have thrown some of my fictional work, and I know, as a literacy expert, fiction and non-fiction are 2 conflicting genres. Regardless, I hope you were able to get my drift.

That is, no matter what your upbringing is or what mistakes & choices you've made in your life, that does not limit where you can reach as a person. Accept what is and what isn't. Most importantly, forgive yourself and soldier on.

I might have been crippled by life not once, not twice, but countless times, yet I was able to dust myself off and soldier on.

A friend once said, *"To fully get back to what you were, including the dreams & ambitions you had for yourself, acceptance of where you are in life is only meant to*

CONCLUSION

strengthen you, so work on that and what you have been blessed with thus far." That, in my eyes, is so rich and powerful.

Napoleon Hill also once said,

> [29] *The vast majority of people are born, grow up, struggle, and go through life in misery and failure, not realizing that it would be just as easy to switch over and get exactly what they want out of life, not recognizing that the mind attracts the thing it dwells upon.*

And just like that, that is the law of attraction in action. Whether you believe it or not, that is how the universe has worked for centuries and centuries; that's how it works today, and definitely how it is going to keep on working.

To my friends & family, hearing some of the things I've written in this book comes as a shock. With my sanity and well-being at stake, I had to. Psychology further goes on to say,

> [30] Many people may find that bad experiences stand out in their memory more than good ones. These memories can intrude on our consciousness even when we do not want them to. This may occur due to negativity bias, which refers to our brain giving more importance to negative experiences.

[31]*Sigmund Freud's* [32]*psychoanalytic theory* emphasizes this.

I believe it is inequitable that society perpetuates the notion that we must

---

[29] *The Secret | Original Bestselling Book by Rhonda Byrne.* (2024, March 6.) The Official Website of The Secret. https://www.thesecret.tv/products/the-secret-book/

[30] Morales-Brown, L. (2023, December 22.) *How to forget unwanted memories.* https://www.medicalnewstoday.com/articles/251655#why-are-bad-memories-so-vivid

[31] https://en.wikipedia.org/wiki/Sigmund_Freud

[32] https://en.wikipedia.org/wiki/Psychoanalytic_theory

wait until we are approximately 40 years old to be qualified to write an autobiography for the benefit of future generations.

Why aren't we able to discuss the future generations of our early twenties? Why do we have to wait until we are only needed to offer guidance? It'll be too late, surely? I believe that one of the most important aspects of growing up is being honest.

And I genuinely believe that future generations can avoid falling into the same mistakes we did by taking a few lessons from our brutal candour regarding our lives to date.

12

Afterword

No one knows what or how one's life should be by 25. But we are familiar with the generational notions of all centuries, "You have to have a degree by 25, have a car, have a stable job, etc."

But what if that was not the case in everyone's life? What if one is still figuring life out, by 25? What if I'm not keen on getting that degree but rather, keen on 'securing the bag' above all? What if the only thing that keeps me going every day is the passion of wanting to be in digital marketing or graphic design, and not getting a doctorate, as my parents wish for their offspring? Am I then regarded as a black sheep of the family or an ambitious individual?

Let's address the elephant in the room: EGO & PROCRASTINATION. From the time you graduate from high school, further on to varsity, you are fed with a lot of paradoxical theories of how to survive in life, but no one addresses the twins, ego + procrastination. Why not? We are too comfortable in our comfort zones.

It's not because one is terrified to take the leap of faith and tap into their creative side of things, but we are scared of starting. I was not experiencing any hardship academically, to be precise, in high school, which made my ego grow more than it should because I had no one in school to calm me down.

Properly. I carried the very same mindset (EGO) to varsity, thinking I was going to sail through, just like I did in high school, and when it dawned on me that that wasn't the case, my marks dropped exponentially, and eventually, I dropped out of my first year. I couldn't take it anymore.

So what? The ego I carried from high school led to procrastination in me lifting a textbook, and instead, I would choose a cold one. Before I could even say anything, my direction shifted, and my life no longer aligned with my friends on campus or back home. Not because of my lifestyle change but because I ran after things out of my reach and timeline, and before I knew it, I flunked out of varsity and chose to get a job. The disappointment I saw in my parents grew into resentment I had for myself, and anything I grew in emotionally didn't matter anymore because of the things in front of me, in front of GRATITUDE, of the things I had acquired before.

I found myself making mistakes after that phase in life, but sometime last year, a friend asked me. What if you are gifted in more than one field? Moreover, I put a star on that message but didn't think about it properly until my birthday. I decided to turn my mistakes into principles.

Here are some of the mistakes turned into principles:

1. *Cash is King, and the King is always in every human being.*
2. *Genuine friendships are automatic; questioning friendship means there is no friendship to begin with.*
3. *Emotional intelligence is, just like your IQ, important.*
4. *Honesty with yourself is hard, but brutal honesty is harder. The only difference is the results, you reap.*
5. *Gratitude is the absence of greed; the two cannot co-exist. One results in peace and tranquility, whereas the other, with a piece in your head, forces you to hate.*
6. *Prevention is better than cure in all aspects of life.*
7. *Never burn bridges. You can't burn a bridge and not come to terms with the*

results.
8. *Listening with true intent is more important than being the speaker.*
9. *Some good things in your life pave the way for bad things to come shortly. Be careful of yourself today, and beware of **everyone's** intentions.*
10. *Discipline is not only telling people you've changed; your results make the loudest noise.*

Now I know you might think I have life figured out, but not even. I still have 4 years to go until I'm 30 years old. Lol. Meet then!

In the interim, take it easy on yourself, and don't forget, YOU MATTER, always.

One love.

13

About the Author

(Njabulo) Nkazimulo Ngidi is the creator of *Mulo Global Studios,* a marketing agency with three years of experience in professional marketing execution. Nkazimulo has helped many brands achieve their online marketing objectives, resulting in increased visibility and return on investment, to mention a few.

Originally from Durban, South Africa, he is an experienced deejay, author, radio host, motivational speaker, customer service leader, and musician. With that said, the author and motivational speaker has made it his life's work to tour the world as a motivational speaker, sharing his wisdom with audiences on topics that have the potential to impact their mental, spiritual, and physical health.

As an autobiographical novelette, this is the author's first published work. He wishes to encourage readers to pursue their goals and to value the gifts, aspirations, and abilities that God has given them. *Nkazimulo* has kept his head up despite his shortcomings, errors, and HIV/AIDS status.

Moreover, the author is a strong proponent of speaking up about one's feelings, particularly when a teenager or young adult, as this is considered the hardest time of a person's life.

ABOUT THE AUTHOR

Message *Nkazimulo Ngidi* on the aforementioned social media platforms for more information.

https://www.facebook.com/n.nkazimulo.ngidi

https://www.linkedin.com/in/nkazimulo-ngidi

https://www.tiktok.com/@nkazimulo_ngidi

https://www.instagram.com/nkazimulo.n.ngidi

www.ingramcontent.com/pod-product-compliance
Lightning Source LLC
Chambersburg PA
CBHW032135090426
42743CB00007B/607